"Deft, clear and
which might as
rassed to ask al
need in the lives

.... by the book."

— Jonathan Lethem, *NYT* bestselling novelist and Roy E. Disney '51
Chair of Creative Writing at Pomona College

"Should be required reading for all writers and editors, as well
as all creative writing teachers and students. Both books are
bursting with outstanding insights and fresh ideas. And as a
bonus, they're written in prose so accomplished and excellent,
they're a lesson in itself on how to write a brilliant writing guide.
Whether you're a newbie beginner or a well-seasoned pro,
these books will make you a better performer, editor and writer."

— Kate Christensen, PEN/Faulkner Award-winning novelist and
former teacher at Iowa Writers Workshop

"James Navé's help is practical, unique and gets to the psych-
ological core. He is encouraging in that most helpful sense: he
shows you how to find your courage. Before I could become a
bestselling author, I had to become an author, and there is no
better coach/advisor/shaman for 'becoming' than Navé. I grew
with his encouragement, guidance and funneling my fog into
focus. He has guided me on how to present myself both on the
page and on the stage."

— Greg Palast, investigative journalist and *NYT* bestselling author

"*How to Read for an Audience* is a book I would recommend to
every author. It's a skill that all writers need help with, particularly
as they begin their careers. Performing in public rarely comes
naturally and this clear and sympathetic guide will swiftly become
an indispensable tool for anyone faced with the challenge of
standing in front of an audience."

— Alexandra Pringle, Editor-in-Chief, Bloomsbury Publishing

ABOUT THE AUTHORS

James Navé has taught creative writing for institutions including the University of Oklahoma, the University of Alabama, Duke University, the National University of Ireland, Galway, and International Schools on five continents. He co-founded the theater company Poetry Alive!, which for over three decades has sent teams of performance readers into schools and colleges to present classic poems, reaching over six million students to date. For eight years he produced Artist's Way Creativity Workshops with Julia Cameron, bestselling author of *The Artist's Way*. He is currently director of the Taos Storytelling Festival and is a founding member of LEAF Community Arts, which hosts the biannual LEAF Festival near Asheville, North Carolina. He is the author of two books, *The Road* (1998) and *Looking at Light* (2012), and holds an MFA in Poetry from Vermont College of Fine Arts. Please visit jamesnave.com.

Allegra Huston is the author of *Love Child: A Memoir of Family Lost and Found*, the novel *Say My Name* (*A Stolen Summer* in paperback) and the DailyOm course "Forgiveness Through Writing," as well as the companion to this volume, *How to Work with a Writer*. For over 30 years she has worked as an editor for major publishing houses in London and New York, including six years as Editorial Director of Weidenfeld & Nicolson, London. She has conducted creative writing workshops for the University of Oklahoma, the National University of Ireland, Galway, the Taos Writers Conference and the UK's prestigious Arvon Foundation. Authors she has worked with include two Nobel Prize winners, three Booker Prize winners, Sir James Goldsmith and Jane Goodall. She holds a First Class Honours degree in English Language and Literature from Hertford College, Oxford. Please visit allegrahuston.com.

"In this book we draw on our combined decades of experience to give you strategies and tools for drawing an audience into your work, as well as advice on handling all the many practicalities of doing a public reading. Between us, we have done hundreds of public events, with audiences ranging from two people in a café/ bookshop to packed auditoriums of over a thousand. We are happy to be able to share what we've learned with you."

Twice 5 Miles Guides
the stuff nobody teaches you

How to Read for an Audience
A Writer's Guide

James Navé and Allegra Huston

Taos • London

Copyright © 2018 by James Navé and Allegra Huston

All rights reserved. No part of this book may be reproduced in any form or by any electronic or mechanical means, including information storage and retrieval systems, without permission in writing from the publisher, except by a reviewer, who may quote brief passages in a review. Scanning, uploading, and electronic distribution of this book or the facilitation of such without the permission of the publisher is prohibited. Please purchase only authorized electronic editions, and do not participate in or encourage electronic piracy of copyrighted materials. Your support of the author's rights is appreciated. Any member of educational institutions wishing to photocopy part or all of the work for classroom use, or anthology, should send inquiries to Twice 5 Miles, P.O. Box 2999, Taos NM 87571, or info@twice5miles.com.

ISBN 978-0-9857528-2-8

Twice 5 Miles
P.O. Box 2999
Taos, NM 87571

twice5miles.com

Book design by Lesley Cox, FEEL Design Associates, Taos NM

CONTENTS

THE VALUE OF READING ALOUD

Are you a writer, promoting your book or magazine work? Are you a poet or storyteller, building your audience? Do you do presentations for your business, internally or externally? Have you been asked to make a speech, at a wedding maybe? Will you be accepting an award?

Are you nervous?

This book will teach you techniques that build both your confidence and your abilities, so that the words you have written make as powerful an impact as possible.

That's not all it will do. If you are a writer, you may already know the value of reading your work aloud as a final step in the editing process. When you read silently, the words just roll along. You wrote them so you know what to expect, and guess what? Your expectations are met. Reading aloud adds a dimension of objectivity. You can hear whether the rhythm of the words is pleasing, where you've repeated a word or a phrase or a grammatical construction.

But when you read aloud with full emotional and intellectual engagement as if you were reading for an audience, you get a far more powerful understanding of your writing. Now you are not just listening to the words; you are feeling them. When you load your writing with its full freight of meaning, conveying it with passion to an empty room, you know viscerally when something feels inauthentic or wrong. You feel the disconnect when you're not actually saying exactly what you want to say.

Practice the techniques explained in the "Rehearse"

section of this book. You will develop your own personal litmus test for what feels right to you, and you will be that much more confident of your writing before you send it out into the world.

Reading work by other writers

Reading written work aloud is like playing music. No matter whether you wrote the song or somebody else did, it's still music. Just as musicians hone their craft by playing the work of other songwriters, not just listening to the recordings, so you can hone your craft by reading the work of other writers aloud and feeling the rhythms in your voice and body.

I (J.N.) have found that reading the work of others, both silently and aloud, memorized or from the page, teaches me more about writing than almost anything. As a performer for Poetry Alive!, I presented poems by Robert Frost, Elizabeth Bishop, Emily Dickinson, Elizabeth Barrett Browning, Robert Browning, Edgar Allan Poe and Robert Service to K–12 students. As my familiarity with these classic poems grew, my own work began to grow and change. Sometimes one of my lines would echo a phrase I'd memorized, or I'd trace the drama in one of my poems back to the tension I'd felt while reading Poe's "The Raven."

Literary fame and healthy sales figures are built by writers who actively promote their work. Yet most writers are thrown into the spotlight with no preparation. No wonder they find it intimidating and unpleasant! No audience wants to watch you doing something you hate, and booksellers will tell you that people walk out of dull readings—which means that writers who don't read well are actively turning potential fans off their work. You do not want that writer to be you.

Fortunately, it's not hard to get good at reading for an audience. And with a bit of time and practice you can get so good that passers-by will stop, listen and even buy your book. That actually happened when I (A.H.) was doing a reading of my novel *Say My Name* at Bookworks in Albuquerque. A woman came into the store to buy something else, was drawn in by my reading and bought not one but two copies of my book (in hardback, even!): one for herself and the other for her sister. (To watch a live-stream of one of my public reading events, visit the Facebook page "Allegra Huston Author.")

And will you believe me when I tell you that before James Navé coached me, I was terrified by public speaking? As an editor at a publishing house presenting my books at sales conferences, my heart would pound, my hands would shake and my nerves drained all authentic enthusiasm out of my voice. I was lucky to work with James Navé before my first book was published, and by the time that book tour was finished I was enjoying an experience I once dreaded. So, I am the poster child for these techniques—and you can be too.

(From here on, "I" refers to James Navé unless otherwise indicated.)

WHAT MAKES A GOOD READING?

Too many writers read in public the way they'd read in private, just saying the words aloud. To engage an audience, you must convey what's strong about your writing: the intensity of the emotion, the beauty of the words and images, the drama of the narrative. We don't mean that you must be theatrical. We mean that you must develop an emotionally connected reading style that reflects your authentic self.

Feelings are transactional. If you feel, your audience will too. The best way to make this happen is to be yourself—and share that self with your audience.

The poet Ocean Vuong, whose book *Night Sky with Exit Wounds* won the T. S. Eliot Prize for Poetry in 2016, is an excellent example of a writer who is comfortable being himself on stage. (To hear him, go to the *New Yorker* website and search "Someday I'll Love Ocean Vuong.") There's nothing histrionic about Ocean. He's soft-spoken, unassuming. When he reads, you feel like he's telling you, and only you, one of his most precious secrets.

When I first met Ocean a few years ago, he was only 21 and just starting out. I was at Bar 13 in Manhattan, at a Monday night reading called Louder Arts. As you might imagine, many poets in that room competed for the imaginary loud prize with vocal volume, gesticulations and general overacting. When Ocean was introduced, he walked slowly to the stage with a small chapbook in his hand. There was something about him that cued the room full of slam poets and spoken word artists to silence.

When he stepped in front of the microphone, he simply said, "Thank you for allowing me to read. I appreciate it."

Ocean opened his chapbook, looked out at us, smiled and began. It was instantly obvious that he was reading from a place deep inside himself. He only read for five minutes. He got a standing ovation.

Unlike Ocean, when I started out with Poetry Alive! I had little awareness of what it meant to be myself on stage. On the contrary, I thought pretending would do the trick. I communicated fear with wide eyes. I frowned for sadness, switched on a smile for happiness. I waved my arms to indicate excitement. But I knew there was something missing. All the emotion in the room was coming from me.

It took a little time for me to realize that I had to stop pretending and fully engage my imagination and my emotions. Then one day, when I reached a place of genuine sadness as I recited a poem—by bringing to mind the death of someone I loved—the students not only believed me, they experienced sadness too. I saw it on their faces. That was when I began to understand what Ocean already knew when he stepped up to the microphone that night at Louder Arts.

In this book, we will show you how to use memory and imaginative circumstances to give emotional depth to your reading. That interior connection will give rise to gestures, facial expressions and variations in your voice, but because they arise naturally they will be authentic— true to you, true to your material.

Apply these techniques, and you will feel the difference immediately. Powerful reading converts listeners (and passers-by) into fans.

GETTING STARTED

Recently the poet Jessica Jacobs called me for help. Her book *Pelvis with Distance* was getting excellent reviews and she was receiving invitations to read her work at bookstores, conferences and universities. She was committed to doing everything she could to get her poems out in public. "I've worked incredibly hard on writing and revising my poems," she told me. "They're regularly published. But every time I'm invited to read, I'm so nervous I do the poems a disservice by not giving myself full-on to sharing my work with an audience. How can I get past my anxiety to allow me to read in such a way that listeners connect with my poems and with me?"

Jessica's nervousness was natural. Most writers are nervous about their first public readings, and for some writers that nervousness never goes away. When we don't know if we can do something, when we haven't received instruction or training, of course we're nervous. As with everything, we get better with practice.

I told Jessica that after she had a few readings under her belt, she'd begin to channel her nervous energy into performance energy. "There are three simple steps," I told her.

Choose your content.
Rehearse.
Show up prepared.

Yes—you will have to rehearse. Even writers who aren't nervous need to rehearse. Just because you wrote the words and can read with confidence doesn't mean you are already able to convey the full emotional impact of your work to an audience. The most common rookie mistakes, which we will discuss on pp. 24–25, are usually the result of a writer not believing they need to rehearse or not knowing how to do it.

If you want to be comfortable in front of an audience *and* read your work with powerful emotional connection, you must commit to a rehearsal process. It demands time that you will have to work into your schedule. We promise you it's worth it. As in painting a room or running a race, preparation is the key to success.

Consider every reading a gift to your audience, yourself and your work. Every rehearsal is a step in creating that gift.

Your audience

When you're nervous about reading in public, you tend to picture the audience as the enemy, distant and judgmental, just waiting for you to mess up. If you think about this for a moment, you'll realize that it's an illusion born of fear. In fact, your audience wants to love you and your work. Some of these people probably already do.

The audience is on your side. They love writing just as you do; that's why they're there. These wonderful people have taken time out of their lives, probably traveled some distance and spent some money, just to hear you read. They've come to witness your imagination at work. They've come to be moved, entertained, motivated, validated, informed, provoked, stimulated and inspired. In short, they're receptive.

They are your allies.

When you stand up in front of your audience, you're making a bargain with them. In return for the effort they've made to be there, you will give them an experience of human connection—though the emotions you share may range from ecstasy to hilarity to rage. This sense of shared emotion—which reminds us that we are not alone, that life is infinitely sad and infinitely sublime, and that there is always something new to fascinate or appall or delight us—is why we read.

Storytellers and speech-givers: skip to p. 23.

PREPARATION 1: CHOOSE YOUR CONTENT

So, what are you going to read? Keep three things in mind as you make your selection:

- Emotional connection
- Timing
- Audience

Emotional connection

Many people in your audience will be experiencing your work for the first time. But they will be hearing your words, not reading them on a page or screen, so they won't have the opportunity to go back and reread, or to slow down in order to understand difficult concepts or ambiguous language. The strongest impact you can make when reading aloud is emotional, not intellectual. For that reason, you will do best if you choose content with which you have a strong emotional connection: passages that make you laugh or cry—if you let yourself.

Pre-select more material than you will have time to read, with a wide emotional range. You're not a robot. You're not going to feel the same way every day, or want to read the same material.

Make your final selection on the day of your reading. If you're going through a difficult time in your personal life, you may want to present material that reflects your emotional state—though if you don't trust yourself to keep control of your emotions, go with something safer. Include as wide a range of emotion as you can manage—or, if it's a short reading, choose material that builds to a powerful climax. Either way, take your audience on a journey.

If your event has a theme, take it into account. Even if you have to stretch to make a connection between the material you want to read and the theme, make sure the connection is there. The organizers will not invite you back if you totally ignore the brief they gave you.

If you are one of two or three readers at an event, you will probably have about 20 minutes (more on timing below). Unless you are an expert at this—in which case, you are probably not reading this book—DO NOT choose one continuous passage or one long poem. You will find it challenging to hold an authentic emotional connection for that long, and your audience's attention is pretty much guaranteed to wander. Instead, choose poems of varying lengths or 3-to-6-minute passages from different parts of your book. For an event in which you are the sole author reading, select five or six passages or 12–15 poems.

For writers of nonfiction

If the appeal of your subject matter is intellectual rather than emotional—such as current affairs, science, technology or history—you might consider a different approach. It's hard to engage listeners with purely intellectual written material, so you must communicate the passion that drives your writing.

Even though you have been asked to do a reading, that doesn't mean all you're allowed to do is read. You may do better to structure your presentation as a talk about your work. For a 20-minute event, condense the story of what you've written to five or six main points and develop a talk that leads your audience along this narrative, or along your journey in writing it. Punctuate each point by reading a paragraph or two. Look for scenes that you've dramatized to help tell your story: moments of discovery, amazing or outrageous truths, unexpected turnarounds, the snatching of victory from the jaws of defeat. (Or the snatching of defeat from the jaws of victory—but, as we'll discuss below, for public readings upbeat is best.) If you can, make 'em laugh.

Your audience's emotional connection to your writing starts with you.

Timing your reading

After you've identified the passages or poems that you might include in your reading, or developed a talk about your writing, the next step is to get an accurate timing. This is where many rookie readers run into trouble: they don't time their reading in advance, they time it inaccurately or they decide it's okay if they run over a bit. Almost always, it's not okay.

Find out how much time you will have for your reading. Open mic slots run 3–6 minutes. Curated multi-writer readings allow 10–20 minutes. Solo events can run an hour or more: usually 30-40 minutes of reading followed by an interview and/or a Q & A.

Staying within your allotted time is one of most professional moves you can make. Less is more. If you have 5 minutes, prepare for 3 minutes. If you have 10 minutes, prepare for 8 minutes. If you have 20 minutes, prepare for 16 minutes. The extra time allows for introductory remarks, pauses, off-the-cuff comments and audience response. If you finish under time, your audience will want more, your fellow readers will appreciate you and your host will ask you to come back.

If you've ever been to an open mic, you've almost certainly seen a reader exceed the time limit. This is not only unfair to the other readers, especially those last on the list; it's unfair to the audience. Some people have come specifically to hear those people who have just been elbowed off the program. Everyone has come to hear a variety of voices. Being greedy, even unintentionally, makes a reader unpopular all around.

Recently a friend was invited to be one of four readers at a local literary society event, each of whom was asked to read for 12-15 minutes. Being a pro, he prepared. The first reader read for 47 minutes of continuous dry prose. The second reader read for half an hour. By the time our friend came on, the audience was bored to tears, fidgety and exhausted. This is the fault of the event's host, of course; it's the host's job to keep things on track, and perhaps the importance of timekeeping should have been emphasized when the invitation to read was made. But even so, do you think those first two readers increased their fan base? Did our friend want to read for that program again?

Most hosts know that bad timekeeping is one of the best ways to kill a reading series. A good host rings a discreet bell or taps a metal bowl when the reader is one minute from time, does the same less discreetly when the reader hits time, and then clangs if they are going on too long. But don't count on your host's generosity; time your reading so that you come in safely under the bell.

Some formats, such as Dime Stories, Pecha Kucha and most poetry slams, have a strict time limit. A noise will sound, or a slide saying "Thank you" will pop up, or the host will firmly reclaim the microphone. If you're not finished, tough. You should have timed it better.

At events where you are the only author reading, running long is less a technical problem than an experiential problem. Audience members with other commitments might start to leave—which breaks the spell for everyone. You've damaged the impact of your writing just because you didn't take your side of the bargain seriously. And the consequences don't end there. People who leave before you've finished, and people who feel that they've heard the whole book because you read so much, rarely take out their wallets to buy it.

How to time your reading

We've often heard people say, "I only have five minutes. If I read fast, do you think I can get through all five pages?" Sure, it's possible if you read like an auctioneer, but you'll lose your audience. It's always better to read less and read it well.

Time your pieces with the stopwatch on your phone. Begin by reading each piece aloud at what seems to be a normal speed. Chances are it will take longer than you expected. If that's the case, trim your material rather than speeding up your pace. As you rehearse, your pace is likely to slow down even further, so cut your selections down far enough to give you room to expand.

Bear in mind that timing is a work in progress. You're going to time yourself again at the end of your rehearsal period, to make sure you're still coming in under the bell, and adjust if necessary. The goal is to finish within your allotted time—but only just. Your audience has made an effort to come and hear you read; you don't want them to leave feeling short-changed.

It's a good idea to have another passage of your

book, or a few poems, in reserve in case you're running short—or, more likely, in case the organizer of a multi-reader event tells you that you have more time just before you go on (because, maybe, another reader hasn't shown up). Prepare for this eventuality. Know where you're going to slot in that extra material. Don't just add it at the end, like an afterthought. Unless, that is, your audience demands an encore.

Your audience

Not all material is suitable for all audiences. If you plan to explore adult themes, make sure this is appropriate for the event. I've been hosting a professional-level poetry slam twice a year for over twenty years at the LEAF Festival in Black Mountain, North Carolina. As you may know, many slam poets make free use of language. Because LEAF is for the most part a family festival, the program always includes a disclaimer that the slam is "for mature audiences only." I repeat that disclaimer from the stage before the show starts and suggest that people with sensitive ears, or who have children with sensitive ears, check out the other shows on offer. You might want to do the same.

If your reading is a 21-and-over event, such as San Francisco's legendary monthly showcase Writers With Drinks, held at a bar called the Make Out Room, consider presenting adult material, if you have it. Your audience will enjoy watching you take a risk. But do this only if you can read the material with confidence! Know that you'll be able to brazen it out without getting embarrassed. If you're uncomfortable—no matter how well you hide it— your audience will be too.

If you know you're going to have children in your audience, choose at least some material that children can relate to. Look for material that features a child character, or subject matter such as friendship or sports that is interesting to people of all ages.

PREPARATION 2: ARRANGE YOUR CONTENT

Fiction and memoir

Select passages that combine to give a sense of your storyline. Don't feel that you have to include every important character, every subplot, every theme. Stick with the main character and perhaps one other. It's usually best to confine yourself to the main plotline (it can take valuable time to explain how a subplot connects in).

Don't choose the climax, or the very end of the book—because if people think they've had the full experience of the book listening to you, they won't buy it. You want to give them an authentic taste of the book; you want to intrigue them; and you want to leave them panting to know how the story is resolved.

Choose for contrast: sad/happy, serious/funny, love/ hate. End on an up beat. If you leave your audience feeling cheerful, they'll be more likely to buy your book and they'll take away better memories of your reading.

Talk to the audience. Just because this is a reading, that doesn't mean that all the words out of your mouth must have previously been written down. You might choose to introduce your reading by saying, for example, "My book [use the title] is the story of a love affair between an older woman and a younger man," and adding any other information the audience might need in order to understand your opening passage. But keep it brief. Get to the actual reading as directly as possible: that is what the audience has come for.

If you're a very confident reader, and your material starts with a bang, you might prefer to launch straight in. If you do, it's still a good idea to include a similar introduction after that first powerful passage. This gives the audience a chance to settle in and absorb its impact before you move on.

Breaking into conversational mode between passages allows the audience to relax their focus for a moment and reset. We've encouraged you to choose for contrast and emotional range, so your audience will need a bit of transition time. This gives you the opportunity to talk a bit about your book—why you wrote it, what you feel passionate about—and to orient the audience before the next passage, with a brief explanation of plot or characters.

Don't give away too much! Limit yourself to what's necessary for the audience to get the emotional impact of the next passage without having to wonder who's who and where they are. Your goal, always, is to enable the emotional connection to be as direct as possible.

If you only have 3-5 minutes, choose one passage that tells a story—or two, maximum three, that fit tightly together without explanation. Go for emotion or narrative suspense rather than plot. Once you have a short-list of possibilities, choose the one that requires the least explanation: who the characters are, what they're doing and so on. You don't have much time, so neither you nor your audience want it spent on talk.

Editing your material

Many writers don't realize that they're "allowed" to make changes to what's on the page. You can leave out words, sentences, even paragraphs, if that serves the reading. The reading is its own thing: it's not "a chunk of the book" or legally binding testimony of its contents. It's an event, and your task is to engage your audience.

What should you leave out?

Wherever possible, omit phrases and sentences that refer to other characters or plotlines that will distract or confuse your audience. And leave out anything that starts to feel inauthentic or clumsy in rehearsal. It happens frequently that you're happy with a passage when you read it over on the page (perhaps you've read it over a hundred times on the page), but when you read it aloud, putting full emotional weight into the words, you realize you're not happy with it at all. If you're uncomfortable with even one word, cut or replace it.

Ideally, you will have done this before your work was

printed and bound between covers. If you didn't know the value of this process back then, at least you know it now. You'll become fascinated by how sensitive your new authenticity meter is.

Poetry

Create a show order, like a band creates a playlist. Too many poets stand at the microphone deciding which poem they're going to read next, forcing the audience to wait while they leaf through pages to see what catches their eye. This is rude. Your audience has made an effort to come and hear you; honor them by showing that you too have made an effort and prepared.

Choose a theme for your reading. This is more for you to work with than to share with your audience, though it's fine to mention it if it seems appropriate. All poets have certain topics they return to, questions they repeatedly explore from new angles, obsessions the subconscious faces them with again and again. As you probably know, it's not wise to dwell on this when you're writing, but an understanding of the energy nodes in your work is an excellent tool when you're planning a reading.

For example, a recurrent theme in your work might be risk, or love, or travel, or betrayal. Settle on one theme. (You can choose a different theme for your next event, which will help to keep things fresh.) Now, select three anchor poems—your strongest poems on that theme— which will go at the beginning, in the middle and at the end. If your allotted time allows for more than those three, slot in other poems that reflect the theme you've chosen. Keep contrast in mind: follow sad with happy, thoughtful with frivolous, desperate with hopeful.

How do you decide which poem goes first, which in the middle and which last? Open strong, but go for intimacy rather than something confrontational. You want to build an alliance with your audience—and if you do happen to have a strongly confrontational poem, it will have more impact if you've wooed your audience first. We will stress often in this book how important it is to create a sense of intimacy with your audience. As we'll discuss on pp. 75–76, material that focuses on "you" makes a strong opening.

You might also select an opening poem based on a sense of beginning, of possibility, of promise or potential, and a closing poem based on a sense of completion, of finality, of wisdom gained or permanent change. If you can, end with a crowd-pleaser (so put that confrontational poem in the middle). When your audience remembers you later, they'll remember the feeling you left them with—and it will be a better memory if it's an upbeat one.

Here's how I might approach the theme of decisions. I'd start with a poem about how I felt rather spare in my twenties because I drove an old pickup truck, so to boost my confidence I bought a Fiat Spyder—not knowing that "Fiat" stood for "fix it again Tony." My middle poem would be about catching a tremendous bass in Enka Lake and deciding to throw it back because I didn't have the heart to make a meal out of the old thing. I'd close with a poem about how I once traded a performance reading for a first-class airline ticket from San Francisco to London.

In this case, I've ordered my three anchor poems on a line of rising success. The first poem describes a bad decision humorously; the second, a decision that makes me feel good but leaves me hungry; the third, a time when I parleyed a skill that I'd worked on (the skill the audience is enjoying at that moment) into a luxury that most of us dream about when we're flying economy.

Depending on the theme, a narrative arc might suggest itself. Let's say you've decided on migration. You might start with a poem about leaving home or striking out for parts unknown, choose a middle poem that tells of an experience you had in a foreign city or a vision quest in the wilderness, and end with a poem that reflects on a journey or summons up a sense of a new home.

If your event already has a theme, respect it but don't let yourself be constrained by it. Allow yourself creative license in choosing your material, and remember that an unexpected take on the theme will add variety to the evening and make your work stand out. If your best poems don't fit neatly into the given theme, see if you can find some oblique way in which they reflect it and come up with a one-liner that makes the connection.

In rehearsal, you will strengthen this connection and nail down the one-liner. Extemporaneous remarks and explanations draw the audience in, as long as they're relevant and brief. They usually work best when they're not truly extemporaneous but have been practiced during rehearsal.

Let's return to the theme of decisions. If three strong poems don't immediately jump to mind, find an angle: another theme that you can tie in to the one you've been given. For example, the themes of decisions and migration overlap: you must decide when to leave, how to leave, where to go. The theme of risk is just as adaptable: every risk is the result of a decision to take it. Or the theme of love: though love may sweep you off your feet, what decisions remain for you to make?

In fact, most themes can be tweaked in many directions.

Write out your show order and a few possible additions. Review it. Does each poem contrast with the ones before and after it, or intensify the mood of the poem it follows? In rehearsal, be aware of whether the transition from one poem to the next feels solid or awkward. Note your instinctive response to each poem. If there's a poem in there that gives you a tired feeling, that you don't enjoy reading aloud even though it's strong on the page, replace it with a poem that may be less strong on the page but more enjoyable to read.

Fiddle with the order until you're entirely happy with it.

Take care that the transitions from poem to poem make narrative sense. For example, Robert Frost's "The Road Not Taken" transitions nicely to Charles Wright's "Lonesome Pine Special," a poem about traveling the blue highways over the landscapes of America. On the other hand, following Elizabeth Barrett Browning's "How Do I Love Thee" with Randall Jarrell's "Death of the Ball

Turret Gunner" creates a clash. Browning declares undying love, while Jarrell describes a ground crew washing a dead gunner's remains out of a Flying Fortress. There's no connection (or maybe there is one that you see and we don't). If this is the kind of juxtaposition you want to make, find a justification for it. Address the question and answer it to your own satisfaction. If you have confidence that it's right, your audience will accept it. You may or may not want to explain this strange juxtaposition to your audience; you can explore this in rehearsal, with one or more partners who can stand in for the audience.

If you'll be reading from a book, use sticky notes to mark the pages, numbering them according to your show order. Use a different color for your three anchor poems. Just seeing that will give you a sense of stability. It will also give you a quick visual to measure your time against. Are you running long or short? Might you have to drop or add a poem or two?

It's helpful to use different colors of sticky notes to code poems that you might drop or add. Seeing where your middle anchor poem is enables you to keep the balance between the first and second halves of your performance.

Once you start to get comfortable reading in public, you might feel like changing your show order on the fly. I call this surfing the audience's mood. If you think you might do this, color-code your poems by emotional tone (upbeat/downbeat) so you can easily find the change of mood you're looking for.

Editing your material

Poets have less scope than prose writers to make changes to the words on the published page. Keep any changes minimal—but feel free to choose sections of a long poem and omit the rest. Of course, if you're reading work by another writer, you don't have license to change it. But if it's your own work, why not improve it if you can? If your book goes into another edition, or your poem is reprinted elsewhere, you'll be able to make the change permanent.

REHEARSE

Are you worried about finding your voice? We'd like to propose that if you have any worries about finding your voice, you can drop those worries now. Your voice is not lost. You have it, and you've had it since you spoke your first word. It's yours. It's unique. Your friends recognize your voice no matter how long it's been since they've heard it.

Yet your unrehearsed everyday voice is not up to the task of a public reading. You may already know that. In our daily lives, we rarely speak with the clarity of meaning and focused, controlled emotion that make a reading powerful. The purpose of rehearsal is to identify and employ the techniques that infuse meaning and emotion into your natural voice.

Before we get into rehearsal technique, let's understand what you *don't* want to do on stage. (We use the word "stage" to refer to the space you occupy when you are presenting your writing in public. It may simply be the area of a room set apart for you, the reader.) The three most common rookie mistakes are droning on, declaiming and hamming it up.

Droning on

A drone is a fixed-pitch pipe of the bagpipes, which sounds a continuous low background tone. It's also a worker bee, and when we say someone is a drone we mean that they are caught in a life of drudgery. "Droning on" recalls both these meanings: an unvarying, low-pitched noise, and being trapped in repetition and tedium.

The newest meaning of the word, a robotic flying machine, underscores the lack of emotion and the unvarying hum.

Almost certainly you've suffered through someone droning on. They step up to the microphone and speak in a monotone, seeming to talk for nobody's benefit but their own. They don't make eye contact with the audience. If they're not actually reading, they're blathering on in some formless monologue.

Declaiming

Declaiming is reading in a loud, artificial voice that insists on the importance of the words regardless of their content. Like droning on, it's an emotion-free zone. For an excellent example of declaiming, go to any courtroom in America and listen to the bailiff announcing the judge.

Hamming it up

Hamming it up is the opposite of droning on and declaiming: it's an overly emotive rendition of your work, inauthentic because it's extreme. Basically, it's bad acting. It's what I did when I first started Poetry Alive!

Hamming it up can be effective if used sparingly. Exaggeration is often funny. Just be sure you don't overdo it.

This may be hard to believe, but I once witnessed the host of a poetry festival manage to drone on, declaim and ham it up all in the same event. As he introduced each reader, he gave a rambling personal opinion of the importance of that poet's work. He then declaimed a few lines in a booming town-crier voice, utterly disconnected from the meaning of the words. He ended each introduction either with a goofy comment about the book's cover design as he waved it around or by ringing a little bell to symbolize that the Muse was on her way.

Trying to show off how smart and talented you are almost always backfires. The cure is to be yourself, connect to your own authentic emotions and speak from the heart.

What is rehearsal?

Rehearsal is what you do in private to prepare for what you will do in public. Everyone rehearses on one level or another. How many times have you gone over what you wanted to say in a meeting while you were sipping your coffee, or how exactly you were going to confess a small transgression to your parent or spouse, or how you might break up with a lover?

You already know that rehearsal means more than just repeating lines over and over until you get them right. That's the rehearsal equivalent of droning on. Why drone when you can play?

Rehearsal is a time for exploration and experimentation. The more time you commit to your rehearsal process, the more you'll expand the boundaries of your comfort zone—and the more comfortable you'll feel on stage.

Commit to your rehearsal

Reading for an audience is a skill you can learn, like playing tennis or dancing the waltz. To gain mastery, you must put in the hours. If you don't practice, you simply won't build the skills it takes to do justice to your work. On the other hand, when you commit to a rehearsal schedule and stick with it, the rest will take care of itself.

Start your rehearsal process at least two weeks before your event, earlier if you can spare the time. Ideally, schedule at least three rehearsals a week. It's better to rehearse for half an hour every few days than for eight hours once a month.

Take yourself seriously. You're preparing for a professional event (even if it's an open mic), and you are entitled to a professional rehearsal period. Blocking out time is the best way to establish a rehearsal schedule. Show up on time for yourself. Adapt your schedule if you must, but don't allow it to be squeezed out by the demands of the day. You'll thank yourself later.

Rehearsal location

Decide where you're going to rehearse. Assign a specific place, somewhere you won't worry about being over-heard. It's important to give yourself the freedom to be as uninhibited as possible. If you're at home, choose a time when nobody else is around or close the door of the room you're in. Maybe put a "Do Not Disturb" sign on it. Turn off your phone. You could also go to a quiet corner of a local park, or borrow a friend's house when they're not home.

Warm up physically and vocally

Your body is your instrument. That's why it's important to warm up before each rehearsal and before you go on stage. If you have a regular physical practice of yoga, walking or going to the gym, do a variation of your work-out warm-up. Be silly, goof around, enjoy it.

Here are some simple warm-up exercises:

- Raise and drop your shoulders a few times.
- Roll your neck in circles to the right and left.
- Do a few knee bends.
- Stretch your arms over your head, repeat.
- Put your hands on your hips and lean left, then right.
- Stick out your tongue like a lion.
- Take deep breaths, hold, exhale.
- Walk around the room while repeating "a, e, i, o, u."

Read your material aloud

You're not going to be reading silently at your event, so don't rehearse silently now.

Stand up. Standing engages your whole body, making you more self-aware (rather than self-conscious). It puts you in the position you'll be in when the event takes place: standing in front of your audience. Standing also helps to get rid of any nervous stiffness.

Now, read aloud each piece you've selected.

On your first read-through, speak more slowly than you would in regular conversation. Take time to notice how you've constructed the sentences or the lines. Don't worry if you stumble over the words—every stumble is a portal into your imagination. Think about the word as you say it again: why did you choose that word and not another one?

On your second read-through, speed up a bit. Feel the narrative momentum that animates the words.

As you continue, play around with pacing. Walk as you read. When you're reading slowly, pretend you're walking through sand. When you're reading at a faster clip, imagine you're sprinting toward a finish line.

Smile as you read. Voice artists use this technique even for things as simple as the warning "Stand clear of the closing doors, please" on the New York subway. Smiling has other benefits, too. It elevates your mood, encourages trust and generates empathy. When you smile, you rise above regret and ease pain. Smiling makes you look younger. It lowers your heart rate and reduces stress. And smiling is contagious: it makes other people feel better too. Therefore, it fosters success.

Please don't resist this by saying that your material is so dark that smiling is inappropriate. If that's true, you're forcing your audience into an endurance contest, not an enjoyable experience. Listen to Jeremy Irons read T. S. Eliot's "The Love Song of J. Alfred Prufrock" on YouTube; even though this is a somber poem about a man who regrets his choices, Irons brings an undertone of ironic humor to his reading.

When you look for the humor, or irony, or acceptance in the work you're reading, you'll notice layers of meaning you might not have realized were there. Make a note of these new layers: take them in, let them percolate in your subconscious. Even if your material is as weighty as "Prufrock," you can still bring your sense of humor to lines like "Do I / Dare disturb the universe?" Well, do you?

Move your body

Let your smile set the stage for your vocal explorations. Even if you're reading about heartbreak, a smile connects you to your authentic emotions. You don't have to be somber to be serious.

Once you get used to rehearsing with a smile, match other body movements to your text. Most of these movements won't appear on stage, but working with body movement in rehearsal keeps your center of gravity near your navel rather than in your head.

Rehearsing is all about being in your body, moving your body and responding to your body—including your head, which weighs about 8–12 pounds. Feel how heavy that is! What a strong neck you have, to support all that weight and hold it in such perfect balance!

Find movements that match the information in your text. Forget subtlety. Be big. Be literal. Being cartoonish works here.

Let's take as an example the line, "I turned left on the two-lane and headed west." Here's how I would move my body to connect with the words. I'd point to my eye with my index finger on "I turned." I'd keep my finger there while I turned my head to the left then stretch my arm in the direction of the imaginary two-lane road.

Body movement activates your imagination. The more you exaggerate your movements now, the more vivid the images in your imagination will become. Don't just picture the two-lane road; admire the sunset, hear the car's wheels on the asphalt. Though these exaggerated body movements will be left behind, the images will travel with you to the stage. This is true even if you stand completely still while reading the piece.

As you read and reread your text while moving your body, layers of meaning will start to emerge. Unlike an onion, which you can peel away to nothing, your imagination is infinite, like a house of mirrors that reflects your image much farther than you can see.

Imaginative circumstances

Imaginative circumstances are the images you bring to mind as you read your work for an audience. Developing these imaginative circumstances is a crucial part of rehearsal.

There's nothing complicated about creating imaginative circumstances. The words are there for you on the page. All you have to do is imagine the sensory experiences that go with them.

If the work you are reading is based on your own life, take yourself back to the moments that inspired it as powerfully as you did when you wrote the words. Remember not just how you felt, but what you saw, what you heard, what you smelled and tasted. Recall the scent of the pine smoke, moonlight shining through the trees, the sensation of sliding your fingers across a clean pillowcase, the feeling you got when you left your car in the long-term lot at the airport, the texture of someone's jacket when you hugged them.

Keep in mind that what you remember is never totally accurate and never complete. Once you accept that you'll never remember perfectly, it becomes easier to be creative with your memories. Let's say you were sitting in a café, listening to the radio. The station might have been WSM, or it might not. Maybe it was June and the night frogs were loud in the trees, or maybe there was a bitterly cold draft coming through the ill-fitting window. Either way, it doesn't matter; all that matters is that you have an abundance of concrete sensory details in your mind.

For each important image, setting or event, settle on three or four landing points. If I'm remembering my mother's hospice room, I might recall the tree with white blossoms outside the window, the music she had playing and the drawings by her grandchildren tacked to the door. As I bring those images to mind during a reading, an internal process will take over that enlivens them further with fluid, atmospheric memories. It's similar to telling a story: you have certain plot points that you know you're going to hit, but each time you tell it, you'll tell it a bit differently.

Let's say you're reading a piece about standing in line to ride the Ferris wheel at the state fair with your younger brother. It was 8:15 pm on a hot August night, with a full moon rising. Your landing-point choices could be your brother's excited face, his buzz-cut hair as you looked down at it, your parents waving as you boarded the ride, sweat making your shirt stick to your lower back. You might remember that you thought the line was long but it moved faster than you expected.

Most of the details will be fairly accurate—but maybe you added that full moon. Generate an abundance of remembered and made-up details, and don't worry about whether or not you'll remember them all when you're reading for an audience. Your landing points will trigger them.

If you'll be performing work by another writer, find something in your experience base that reflects the environment and emotional circumstances of the piece. Let's return to Jeremy Irons's reading of "The Love Song of J. Alfred Prufrock." What do you think Irons was thinking about as he spoke the lines "Shall I say, I have gone at dusk through narrow streets / And watched the smoke that rises from the pipes / Of lonely men in shirt-sleeves, leaning out of windows?" Was he remembering a time when he took a lonely walk through a narrow street at dusk? Or the season, the air temperature? He might have been imagining walking home to an empty apartment, or remembering people he'd encountered over the years on lonely walks. Perhaps he was recalling a time when he leaned out a window, waiting for someone.

As you dig into your memories, you'll remember details you thought you'd forgotten. Ask yourself questions. What experiences in your life might be reflected in the words you're reading? Delve into the inventory of your emotional memory.

The more you work with imaginative circumstances in rehearsal, the more easily they'll arise and synchronize with your words when you're standing in front of an audience. The collage of your memories will infuse your reading with authenticity and emotional truth. The process is both conscious and not conscious: you consciously intend it and you have consciously created the circumstances that enable it to happen, but when it happens it happens organically, without conscious effort.

Even though your audience isn't aware of your internal process, they are affected by it. The more real your imaginative circumstances are for you, the more engaged the audience will be in your story. They will feel excitement, relief, joy, fear, doubt, uncertainty, expectation, happiness and curiosity. Images will rise up for them as your words blend with their memories: they will see their own Ferris wheels and hospice rooms, smell the sage or the exhaust fumes or the summer rain, feel the breeze that's lifting the curtain, hear the jangle of carnival music.

Once you make your choices of imaginative circumstances, stick with them. Trust them. They will give you a permanent foundation to build on. You'll also notice that you're developing a more intimate relationship with your text. For me, when I rehearse, it's like I'm slow-dancing with my poem to an old song at closing time.

Let your instincts come out to play

This is rehearsal: you're allowed to do anything! Not just allowed—encouraged. Commanded, even. Nobody's watching; or if they are, they're on your side and they just want you to go bigger, bolder, more extreme.

Be playful, adventurous, improvisational. If you're a casual dresser, buy a wild scarf at the thrift store and wear it with sassy boots while you rehearse.

Walt Whitman wrote, "I am large, I contain multitudes." So do you. Stretch your emotional and physical range. Pretend you're a bear walking in the forest in November, stuffed with berries, or in April, grumpy and hungry after a long hibernation. Pretend you're a mouse creeping around the kitchen at midnight. Try character voices: pretend you're a forced-to-be-happy tour guide, a frustrated carpenter, a thrilled lottery winner. You won't be pretending when it comes to your actual reading, but explorations such as these will add variation and impact to your words, making the chance that you'll drone on or declaim very slim indeed.

Play with your persona. We don't mean put on a fake one, but see if you can find an aspect of your personality that doesn't come out very often—or that goes into hiding when you think about your upcoming event. Possibly the elements of your personality that come out when you read for an audience are the shy, nervous, introverted, anxious ones. Playful rehearsal will put you in touch with the more confident, outgoing, entertaining aspects of yourself.

When you throw your full body into your rehearsal process, expect your creative instincts to start broadcasting a plethora of lucid thoughts, ideas and directions. In fact, you could say that your body is its own director, in the same way that health professionals will say that your body is its own physician. Trust your director. Your creative instincts are as much a part of you as your little toes and all the rest of that wonderful body you call yours.

All of your rehearsal ideas are valuable, even the ones you think might not work. I felt foolish the first time I used a little brown stuffed lion named Boris to work on dialogue. How childish, I thought. Perhaps so—but years later, Boris is still on the job. You'd be surprised by how many characters he can play.

Develop your vocal range

Once you start synchronizing your voice with your body movements and your imagination kicks in, you'll start to notice natural inflections emerging in your voice. Big body movements will amplify your voice. Restrained gestures will soften it. If you're playing with character, you might drop or rise a few registers from your normal speaking voice.

Experiment with the tonal range of your voice: high, low, squeaky, commanding, beseeching, questioning, and so on.

Running scales is another good way to increase your vocal range. Try it. Say the notes of the scale, "do, re, mi, fa, sol, la, ti, do," and go up a step with each one. You don't need to actually sing them. Go slow. Go fast. Enunciate each syllable while exaggerating the movements of your mouth.

You'll notice that your face and throat get tired after you run the scale a few times. The muscles that move your mouth and vocal cords will grow stronger if you exercise them. You can find lots of vocal exercises online; I like the ones on the website of the American Academy of Otolaryngology–Head and Neck Surgery: google "Vocal Warmup: Put Your Best Voice Forward."

Enunciation

Enunciation means speaking words clearly without muttering, mumbling, slurring or sputtering around. We're not suggesting that you pronounce your words like an old-fashioned English actor, nor that you drop your regional accent, if you have one. Your accent makes you sound like you. We're saying only that it's important to speak clearly enough so that your words are easy to understand. This is why we suggested you practice enunciating the syllables of the scale.

If you're not sure whether your enunciation is clear, ask a trusted friend. A little online research will turn up plenty of exercises you can incorporate in your rehearsal. I like the wine cork exercise. Here's how it works. Find yourself a cork, real or plastic, doesn't matter; either way, it will be malleable enough not to break when you bite into it. Put the cork between your front teeth. Bite down. Now read your piece aloud.

The only downside to this exercise is that you'll drool while you're doing it. But what's a little drool when the end result is clarity? The upside is that the cork forces you to pronounce each syllable as a stand-alone utterance. Do this every day for a few weeks and you'll find that your normal speaking voice becomes stronger, clearer and more compelling. You'll also get really good at tongue-twisters.

Voice projection

I once went to a poetry reading in Cambridge, Massachusetts, at which a stately professor with thick black hair mumbled into the microphone for ten minutes. Finally, somebody at the back called out, "We can't hear you!"

The professor looked up, pushed his hair back, leaned into the microphone and said with proper voice projection, "That's your problem." Then he went back to mumbling his poetry.

Obviously, this is not a good way to popularize your work. Your audience will enjoy it more if they can hear it.

Voice projection enables you to be heard clearly and comfortably, whether or not you are using a microphone. (We'll discuss microphones on p. 58.) It is more than just talking loudly. It's certainly not shouting. In fact, you can use voice projection even while whispering. When you project your voice it sounds normal but strong, because it is reverberating in the cavities of your head and that amplified sound is broadcast into the room.

A voice coach or singing teacher will school you in this technique. If you cannot afford to hire one, follow these steps:

1. Put your hand on your head. Relax. Take a deep breath. Let your breath out slowly.

2. Keep your hand on your head. Relax. Take a deep breath. Hum and feel your head vibrate as you let your breath out slowly.

3. Keep your hand on your head. Relax. Take a deep breath. This time, add words and feel your head vibrate as you let your breath out slowly.

Practice this three times a day until you feel the technique becoming natural. Vibrate your head whenever you have a conversation and during your rehearsals. If you find yourself in a sizable empty room, try it out. See if you can hear your voice bouncing off the far wall. A good mental image is to think of your voice as a beach ball flying over your audience's heads and falling three feet behind the back row.

Keep these tips in mind also:

- Include the rafters when you fill up a room with your voice.
- Use good posture; stand up straight.
- Drink plenty of water.

Identify your weaknesses

Identify particular weaknesses or habits that you want to work on. Even though I've been doing a memorized performance of Dylan Thomas's "A Child's Christmas in Wales"—an excellent example of poetry, prose and storytelling rolled into one—every December for over twenty years, I still rehearse it. Since I tend to move my arms about and wander unnecessarily on stage, in one rehearsal I tied my wrists to a chair with yoga straps. Being still helped me to imagine the heavy snow swirling out of the sky; it gave me the quietness to visualize the "birds the color of red-flannel petticoats" as they "whisked past the harp-shaped hills."

That afternoon, I was rehearsing with Christy Ferrato and Tish Vallés, both accomplished poets and excellent readers. I'd asked them to give me directorial feedback; the yoga straps were Tish's idea. This is an example of how rehearsing with others can influence your process in a way that can't happen if you're alone.

Rehearsing alone and with others

You can choose to rehearse alone, with a single partner or with a small group of other writers. Each has its advantages, so experiment with all three.

Alone: You are not dependent on someone else's schedule or reliability. If your own schedule is busy, it may be easiest to slot in time alone. You may feel more free to play and explore if nobody is watching.

With practice, you'll be able to tell for yourself if your material is unclear, or repetitive, or badly arranged. But if you're a beginner at reading in public, enlist help. Even if you prefer to rehearse alone, schedule at least one rehearsal with a trusted friend. There is no substitute for a real live listener telling you what is powerful and what needs more work.

With a partner or partners: Committing to rehearsal partnerships with one or more people raises the stakes and makes you want to do more. As with the yoga straps, rehearsal partners can push you to do things you might not think of or would feel silly or incapable of doing alone. Most importantly, they can stand in for your audience and reflect back to you the impact of your reading.

Working with a partner also allows you to employ more advanced rehearsal techniques, the kind professional actors and directors use. We've had great success with a technique we call "drawing it out of the reader." You can watch video of this at twice5miles.com. But before you establish that kind of intimacy, you have to establish a trust. It's vital that you, the reader, know that the coach has your best interests in mind and is interrupting because he or she wants more and knows you can connect more deeply as you speak. Without trust, the technique risks being authoritarian; with trust, it's like an exciting dance, the kind that makes you collapse laughing in a heap when the music ends.

Ground rules for rehearsing with others

- Respect everybody's creative process. Be mindful that everybody approaches the work in their own way.
- Understand that you are all there to help one another. Nobody is the director. You direct one another. Nobody knows best. Everyone shares their impressions.
- Listen. Be quiet when others are speaking, and pay attention.
- Show up promptly, prepared and ready to work. Don't waste other people's time.

- Make sure your rehearsal space is clean. If it's cluttered, straighten it up a bit.
- Divide the rehearsal time evenly among the readers.
- Ask each reader how they would like feedback to be given: "If I feel you're going off track, would you like me to stop you or would you rather run all the way through? What works for you?"
- Focus on what's good. Be specific about moments when you were moved by what you heard.
- Couch negative feedback in terms of what could be better rather than what's wrong.
- Whenever anyone throws out an idea, say yes to it. Tying my wrists to the chair is a good example of this.
- Respect start and finish times. If you want to add more time, get everyone's agreement.

Pulling it all together

We've encouraged you to let your rehearsal process be messy, improvisational and creative. As your event approaches, you'll need to rein the exploration back in, keeping what's useful and discarding what isn't.

We recommend that you dedicate approximately half of your rehearsal schedule to exploration. Dig into each piece individually, discover what makes it tick, find your points of emotional connection and develop your imaginative circumstances. You'll know you have it together when you're able to read it aloud feeling really comfortable and fully connected emotionally. If you're not sure you've reached that point, invite a few trusted friends to a dress rehearsal.

Very experienced performers will continue to dig right up to the date of the reading and even during it. This is how they keep their material fresh. Only try this once you feel confident on stage. The poet and story-teller Minton Sparks has an interesting technique. Just before she begins to read, she chooses a body part and performs the piece through it: her right knee, her left ear, her left little toe. Try this in rehearsal and notice how striking the differences are.

In your remaining rehearsals, run your reading in its entirety. Include any explanations, digressions and conversational remarks you plan to make.

Linking material and conversational remarks

Most readings will include at least a few sentences that aren't part of the work you're presenting. You don't have to write out this material, but it's important to practice it. Don't think, during rehearsal, "and then I'll explain that she's now in Chicago"; explain it. Refine the explanation by saying it over and over again.

As you rehearse, you'll feel your presentation become tighter, more coherent and more natural. You'll feel more confident. You won't ramble and you won't find yourself fumbling for words or leaning on verbal crutches such as "uh," "you know" and the dreaded "like." Your conversational remarks will come out with zest and zing. You'll say exactly what you want to say, and no more.

Impromptu comments are a terrific way to connect with your audience, as long as you don't chatter on. You'll develop this skill over time, but in the beginning it's safer to rehearse your comments. If you feel moved to add something further during your event, go for it—that's the only way you'll learn. Just keep it short!

Remember, you're under no obligation to say anything between pieces. It's perfectly fine for a confident, deliberate silence to be your bridge. Your audience will appreciate and understand.

Movement vs. stillness

When I first started reading for an audience, I compensated for my nervousness by striding to the microphone like an action figure. My busy, hurried movements helped me keep my guard up. Somewhere along the way, I began to realize that my movements were creating a barrier between me and my audience. That's when I started to experiment with standing still and holding silence. I was pleasantly surprised when people came up to me after the show with comments like, "Thank you, I loved the way you held silence while standing still. It made me feel included."

Movement is distracting because it's a magnet for attention, as any sleight-of-hand artist will tell you. It gives control of the watcher's eyes to the person who's being watched. When you stand still, with no veneer of busyness or attitude, you control the moment but not your watchers. They feel this freedom and appreciate it. You open yourself and your audience to a reciprocal vulnerability. You are saying to them, I am human just as you are. You create a space in which they can give themselves over to the emotions your work calls up in them. You create intimacy. (More on intimacy on pp. 75–80.)

Fortunately, standing still requires very little practice. Try it now. Rise from your seat. Find a comfortable upright posture. Now, stand still for a minute. Notice how your good posture allows your head to balance with ease on your neck and shoulders. Call this your confident stance.

Now give it a try in front of a group or in front of a mirror. The first time you do it, you may feel vulnerable. Stick with it until you experience yourself dropping your guard and a strength welling up inside you. This is the strength that will ground you during your reading.

If this doesn't happen the first time, keep practicing. I promise you it will.

Recently I attended a breakfast lecture series called Creative Mornings in Asheville, North Carolina. The speakers were informative and entertaining. But within less than a minute, every single one was wandering back and forth like a tiger in a cage. Now, that tiger has a good reason for pacing back and forth: it wants out. "Tiger in a cage" is not the impression you want to give.

Just like your words, which you've carefully rehearsed, movement should be the result of intention. It should have a purpose—which may be simple, such as a change of position so that a different section of the audience can see you better. Before you take a step, know why you're taking the step. If there's no good reason for your movement, don't make it. If there is a good reason, you won't be wandering aimlessly but walking with a purpose. When you move your arms, you won't be flapping around but making a gesture that's relevant to your text.

Practice this in rehearsal so that when you find yourself moving unnecessarily during your presentation, you can reel yourself back in.

All movement begins with stillness. Stillness suggests calmness, which communicates confidence. It focuses the audience's attention. A still face with a tear on the cheek is always more dramatic than wailing and flailing.

And that's not all. Stillness also functions as a launch pad for your audience's imagination.

Practice looking up from the page

One of the best ways to connect with an audience is to make eye contact. It's also far easier to do if you're standing still. But if you haven't practiced looking up from the page during rehearsal, you may not feel comfortable doing it during your reading—and you risk losing your place.

The more you practice looking up from the page, the more you'll start to notice the natural thought beats in your text. These are the points where you can raise your eyes and look at your audience. Every piece of writing has thought beats. Rehearsal will make them obvious to you. Once you've identified the look-up points in your text, mark them with a colored pen, using a different color for each look-up point. This simple strategy ensures you will never lose your place.

Time your reading again

Almost certainly you've slowed down from when you first timed your pieces, and you may have added linking material. This is good news, though you may have to do a bit more trimming. Don't regret that you can read less material! Be glad that the pieces you will read have space to expand in, so the audience will have time to connect fully with each one.

Be strict with yourself. Don't run over! You don't need to leave as much wiggle room as in your first timing, but you still need to leave some if the event format demands an exact finish time. Make sure that unpredictable things such as a microphone that needs to be adjusted, or a siren in the street outside, or audience laughter, don't send you over the mark.

Nervousness

If the imminent prospect of your reading is still making you nervous, explore your nervousness. Not everyone's nervousness is the same. Get to know yours. Does it have a color? What animal would it be? What does it sound like if it doesn't have words? Where does it come from? Might it like to go back there?

A good idea is to find a talisman whose purpose is to comfort your nervousness. When it's in your pocket, you know you'll be fine. The downside is that you might lose or forget your talisman. Many people use a talismanic thought instead. You might picture a departed parent or mentor looking down on you with love and protecting you. Or you might do a short meditation in which you imagine yourself in a place of serenity before you step into the spotlight.

If you treat your nervousness as an enemy or try to ignore it, it will waylay you. Instead, try looking at it as energy you can channel. Many actors and public speakers will tell you that nervousness is like a crude oil they have learned to refine into high-octane fuel. Refining your nervousness into high-octane fuel might seem a bit out of reach if you're still a beginner at this. That's understandable. Most likely you equate your nervousness with fear, as many people do—which, again, is understandable. But what, really, are you afraid of? Reading your work for an audience is qualitatively different from being stuck on a crumbling ledge 500 feet above a canyon.

You believe in your work; if you didn't, you wouldn't be reading it in public. It's true that you don't know how the audience will receive it, but the chances are they'll like it. That's what they're expecting, otherwise they wouldn't be there. They don't want to have wasted their time. As we've said more than once in this book, the audience is your friend.

Like your audience, your nervousness is your ally, not your enemy. What is it telling you? Perhaps to run over your show order again or check that you remembered your reading glasses. Perhaps you're dehydrated or a little hungry. Perhaps your nervousness is asking you to focus on the room, to notice what's outside yourself, to connect with the audience. It could be just reminding you to smile.

Though we've given you what we hope are some new

thoughts, they won't make your nervousness suddenly vanish. But see if they help you alchemize your nervousness. Take a deep breath and relabel that pounding heart and sweaty palms with terms like excitement, anticipation, courage and pride.

*

Rehearsal—whether or not you have an event coming up—can become an ongoing practice, like meditation or journaling. Writers who do frequent public readings follow a rehearsal schedule whether they have an event booked or not, ensuring that they are always performance-ready in case a last-minute opportunity arises. A regular practice will make you a fantastic public speaker—a skill you can use for the rest of your life in many situations. Lucky you.

SHOW UP PREPARED

You've chosen your material, timed it accurately, developed your voice and your reading techniques. Are you ready for your event? Not quite.

Book sales

If you have a published book, find out as soon as possible who is in charge of book sales: you or the venue. If the venue is a bookstore, you don't need to give it further thought; they're pros. If it's a performance space with a store attached or any other kind of non-bookstore venue, you'll need to check on a few things:

- Are they ordering books? (They may need up to a two-week lead time.) If so, have they ordered enough? Consider bringing some extra.
- If you are bringing books for them to sell, how will you receive your share and what will it be?
- Can they take credit cards?

If you are handling sales yourself:

- Make sure you have enough books, and a sturdy box to carry them in.
- Sign up for a payment app such as Square. Allow enough time for the card reader to arrive by mail, and hook up the app to your bank account.
- Set a price. It doesn't have to be the publisher's suggested retail price. Choose a round number, ideally a multiple of $5. Making change takes time.
- Ask the venue to assign a table for book sales and signing.
- Enlist a friend to handle payment, so that you are free to sign books and chat with your audience.

Your book sales table should *always* have a sign-up sheet for your mailing list.

Mailing list sign-up sheet

You'll get more sign-ups if the form looks professional. Don't just use a hand-scrawled piece of paper, or a page in your notebook. Create an attractive, typed form with a heading, and put it on a clipboard. Attach a pen to the clipboard with a long string. If you dislike that, bring at least five pens.

You want a name, an email address and a home location so that you can notify people of further events in their area. Asking for too much information puts people off, so keep it minimal.

You can download a mailing list sign-up sheet at twice5miles.com/downloads.

Mark up your reading copy

If the work you're presenting is in a published book, it looks better to read from a bound copy than from loose pages. I (A.H.) use a proof copy of my book as my reading text, so that it doesn't get mixed up with the finished copies for sale.

However, if you can't read the book easily—and be prepared for low or glaring lighting—make an enlarged photocopy or retype your material double-spaced in a large enough font. If you are bent over the text peering at the words, your performance will suffer.

If you're reading from a bound copy, your edits should be made straight onto the page. Use pencil in case you might want to change them, but be aware that the lighting in some venues can make pencil hard to see. Mark the beginnings and endings of your passages with sticky arrows or strong lines that your eye won't have to search for.

Flag the pages where your passages begin so that

you can find them easily. (If you're a poet, you've already flagged them during rehearsal.) Here are two methods:

- Turn down the corners of the pages. Fold them over a few times, big folds, so that they're super easy to locate. *Disadvantage:* you can't number them, so this works best if you're reading in sequential order.
- Use sticky notes. *Disadvantage:* more than a few look messy, and they can get detached. To prevent this, put the book in a ziplock for its journey to the venue.

Before every reading, make sure that you can go straight to the passages or poems you're going to read. You've probably rehearsed other material too, which you'll read on other occasions, but you don't want to be fumbling through thickets of sticky notes or searching a number of pages to find your next piece. So unfold any extra folded pages, and either use color-coded stickies or remove the ones you don't need.

Decide what to wear

As the designer and stylist Rachel Zoe says, "Style is a way to say who you are without having to speak." Dressing well on stage boosts your confidence, communicates respect for your audience and says, without overstating it, that you take yourself and your work seriously. This is the case even if your venue is a café or private home. Consider how different it feels to wear a pair of well-made Italian shoes versus flip-flops. Flip-flops may be appropriate if you're reading something beachy or if they're part of your signature look, but if they undermine the sense that this is a special occasion, choose something else.

Start out by wearing stylish yet straightforward clothes in medium to dark tones. Blue is your best bet; it reminds people of the sky, or a body of water, or the blue bird of happiness. Blue is flattering on camera.

Red can offer your audience a festive visual experience, especially if you wear red shoes to match, though it isn't as effective on camera as blue. Some people will tell you to avoid black for a stage event because its weighty energy can make you look like a phantom shadow, but if you habitually dress in black, it's better to feel like yourself than to feel like you're wearing some kind of costume. White can glare in photographs. Make sure that you're not wearing the same color as your backdrop, such as a black, blue or red auditorium curtain. You'll disappear.

You might want to develope a signature look, which will become part of your brand. Some writers are known for wearing a scarf or a gorgeous embroidered jacket on stage—but if you wear one dramatic piece, keep the rest of your outfit simple. For an excellent example of a well-developed stage style, google the Avalon Jazz Band. The group's musical inspiration and snappy style come from the "swing kids" of World War II Paris known as zazous.

Dress down if that's your style, but keep it sharp, not frumpy. Avoid clothes with screen-printed images or text unless your reading is promoting a cause. Above all, be aware of the messages your clothing sends. All clothing sends messages. If you're not sure what your clothes are saying, ask friends whom you trust to tell you the truth.

When you dress well, people notice and remember. Your odds go up that they will snap photos of you and share them on social media. But don't overdo it. This is not the time to look like you're in costume or to wear something so eye-catching that the audience can't concentrate on your words. Your outfit should complement, not upstage, your reading.

And decide in advance! Your outfit is not what you need to be spending energy on just before the event. Make sure you're comfortable. Clothing that's too tight will make you feel restricted, not expansive. If you'll be standing for an hour or more, do you really want to wear high heels?

Pack your bag

What do you need to bring with you? Make a checklist, or download this one at twice5miles.com/downloads. It might include:

- Reading glasses
- A change of clothes in case you spill something on your outfit
- Mints to freshen your breath
- A bottle of water

- Your preferred pen, if you'll be signing books
- Books or other merchandise to sell
- A credit-card reader and/or cashbox, if you'll be handling book sales yourself, along with cash for making change: $20 in dollar bills, $25 in fives and $20 in tens
- A sign-up sheet for your mailing list, with pen or pens
- Your phone or other recording device, and any accessories such as a stand, elastic bands, charging cord and extension cord. (We'll discuss live-streaming on pp. 88–89.)

Consider keeping the things you need for readings in a dedicated bag, so they're always ready to go.

ARRIVING AT THE VENUE

Aim to arrive at least half an hour early, more if it's an auditorium with a stage. This gives you the opportunity to familiarize yourself with the room's layout and lighting and make adjustments if possible, and generally make sure you're not going to be taken by surprise if you can help it.

When you arrive, locate your host. This may be the bookstore or café manager, or an emcee. Find out who will be introducing you. You may want to ask if you can read their introduction in advance, in case a publicist has provided them with out-of-date information. This happens frequently.

The stage

Most venues won't have an actual stage. The place where you will be standing, or sitting, functions as a stage. It should have a certain amount of space around it, to make it feel set-off and special. Perhaps the lighting will be stronger. There may be a bookstore or event banner behind you. There may be a podium.

Do you actually want a podium? Some readers prefer it, but it can make you feel like a professor lecturing to a classroom. You can ask for it to be removed. If it can't be removed, you're not obliged to stand behind it as long as you don't need to use a fixed microphone.

If your venue is an actual classroom, do whatever you can to counteract the sense of teacher and students. Maybe you can perch on a desk and avoid the "teacher" spot altogether.

Do you prefer to stand or sit? We recommend standing if you are alone on stage, sitting if there are two of you in conversation. If you'll be reading first and then in conversation with someone, decide whether that person will sit on stage and watch you read or wait to come on stage once you've finished. The best option is usually for them to wait to one side while you stand and read, then when they join you on stage you both sit down. This creates a nice break, and lets momentum build again.

Do you know where you'll be signing books afterward? You'll want to be able to walk straight to that spot when you leave the stage, without having to ask or wander around. Assign a table, if possible; it's awkward signing books in midair.

Changing the room

Many venues, such as bars, clubs and auditoriums, don't allow you to rearrange the seating. Bookstores, galleries, cafés and private living rooms have varying degrees of leeway.

In an informal venue, you'll probably find the chairs and stage set up when you arrive. If the venue has hosted similar events in the past, the configuration will probably work well. That said, it's fine to ask for the chairs to be moved to suit you—for example, if you find the front row too close or too far from where you'll be reading.

Occasionally, you'll arrive at a venue which isn't set up, such as a café or a private home. In a gallery or other occasional venue, you may find rented chairs stacked against the wall, the microphone unconnected to its stand and amplifier, no table for book sales. One of the advantages of an un-set-up venue is that you have a chance to feel out the room and decide where you want the stage to be. The people at the venue will follow your lead if you take charge with confidence.

Your reading position should command the room. If possible, move or block off any seating that will be behind or on either side of you. If you're in a gallery, choose a spot with a blank wall immediately behind your head, as an artwork may distract from the images you're calling up with your words. It will also be confusing in photographs.

In many bookstores and cafés, you'll find the stage area in front of a window. Bookstores are usually locked into their setup due to the necessity of moving shelving to make space, but a café or gallery might allow you to change the configuration. If you can, avoid standing with your back to a window, as it will upstage you with reflections from the room at night or action outside during the day. In a café, find an area as far from the counter as possible; even if nobody's making coffee (and they better not be!), there's far too much visual distraction.

Make the stage area as visually appealing as possible. If, for example, a floor lamp and your microphone are standing side by side, move the lamp to a corner.

Lighting

Every venue has a different lighting configuration. Some bookstores will have floor lamps; others will have overhead lights. Auditoriums will have theater lights. Cafés will probably have track lighting. Classrooms will have natural light or fluorescents.

If you're in a venue where the lighting can be adjusted, ask someone whether the lighting on the stage area flatters you or makes you look washed out; you don't want to look like you've just risen from the grave in the Instagram photo. Most importantly, make sure your audience can see you. If possible, make the lighting over the stage area a little brighter. Look for dimmer switches and movable floor lamps, or see if turning off one track of lighting improves things.

Your light check should cover the whole room, not just the stage. For example, if you're doing an afternoon show in a place with west-facing windows, the sun may dazzle you or your audience. Lower the blind, if there is one. If there isn't, adjust the room setup if you can.

In formal venues such as community theaters, the venue manager may take a theatrical approach, lighting the stage while leaving the house lights dark. This is not the best arrangement for a reading, as your goal is to connect with the audience on a personal level and it's hard to do that when you can't make eye contact. Venue managers are generally cooperative, so ask if the house lights can be brought up. Ideally, the house lights will be dim enough to create a distinction between stage and audience but bright enough so that you can see people's faces.

College lecture rooms are the most unforgiving. Get the overhead lights dimmed if possible, but the chances are you'll just have to work with what you've got.

Above all, make sure that there will be enough light for you to read by. At Writers With Drinks, which is held in a bar, I (A.H.) had to use the flashlight on my phone. Fortunately I'd checked this out before the show started, so when I reached the stage the flashlight app was on and ready to go.

Using a microphone

Most venues have a microphone—but just because it's there doesn't mean you have to use it. A fixed microphone may require you to hold the book unnaturally high, which interferes with the audience seeing your face. A hand-held microphone occupies the hand you'll need for turning pages. Either one gives you another thing to think about: managing the microphone or staying close enough to it. If you have worked on voice projection, you should be able to do a reading in a bookstore, gallery or café without amplification. As long as you can be clearly heard, the audience will prefer your natural voice.

A microphone is a tool that enhances your voice projection. Think of it as a resonance chamber for your voice, similar to the cavities in your head. As demonstrated by the example of the mumbling professor above, it does not replace voice projection. If you mumble, a microphone will just make your mumbling louder.

Here's how it works. Just as your vocal cords convert the air from your lungs into vibrations, a microphone converts those vocal vibrations into electrical signals, which travel through a soundboard before being amplified through speakers. Most microphones are unidirectional, which means they pick up sound from one direction only. You have to speak directly into them. No two microphones are the same; they all have quirks. You'll feel more comfortable if you've test-driven the microphone before your reading starts.

Find the on-off button on the microphone itself, and turn it on. Your mouth should be 4–6 inches away from it; you can measure this with a hand span. Read a line or two from your text, pitching your voice both high and low.

If you'll be holding the microphone, figure out how you're going to turn the pages. Don't let a hand-held microphone take you by surprise.

Your sound check should also include the microphone stand, if there is one. Can you set the height beforehand or will it have to be adjusted after a previous reader? Will the host make the adjustment or are you expected to do it? Microphone stands have quirks too, so if you'll be doing the adjusting yourself, test the clamps. Some are stiff; some are loose. Old microphone stands are often hard to adjust, and I've seen more than one fall apart on stage. Better to be aware of this danger in advance.

A fixed microphone severely limits your movement. If you are above it, under it, on either side of it, closer than 4 inches or further back than about 10 inches, you won't be clearly heard. If you are going to be doing readings in large venues where microphones are necessary, consider investing in a wireless head-worn microphone. Since it loops over your ear and sits in front of your mouth, you can speak and move naturally. A mid-range head-worn microphone costs around $500.

And finally ...

Here's a checklist of what you should do before your reading starts. You may want to add items of your own.

1. Turn off your phone!
2. Identify where you'll enter the stage and walk to your position. Be aware of anything that might make you trip.
3. Place a bottle or glass of water where you'll be able to reach it.
4. Locate the entrances and exits, so that you won't be startled by someone arriving late through an unexpected door.

5. Set up any recording device.
6. Place your mailing list sign-up form on the signing table.
7. Review the stage from the back of the room, to make sure there's no random door accidentally left open or other visual distraction.

You can download this checklist, along with the packing checklist and email sign-up form, at twice5miles.com/downloads.

IT'S SHOWTIME, FOLKS

Your entrance

Your public event begins as soon as the first audience member sees you. Be aware of how you present yourself from the moment you enter the venue until the moment you leave it. Good posture expresses confidence. A friendly face makes the audience warm to you.

You will probably be at the venue ahead of time, so you will greet people as they arrive. Thank them for coming. Ask them how they heard about your event and what drew them in.

If your turnout is much lower than expected and people have scattered themselves across the available seating, invite them to move closer in. Maybe even re-arrange the chairs in a circle. Ideally the host will do this, but if the host doesn't, go ahead and do it yourself. People like to sit in circles; it brings back our ancestral days around the campfire, telling stories.

When the host is ready to start, move to one side or take your seat. Keep your good posture, 360-degree room awareness and feet planted firmly on the floor. Take a drink of water. Have your finger marking the page where you'll begin your reading.

What if only two people show up?

It happens. Don't complain! It ruins the evening for everyone. Be grateful that these two people made the effort to come and hear you. Show them your gratitude by taking them as seriously as you would a larger audience. Smile at them, make eye contact as you read. They are getting what amounts to a private reading. If a billionaire was your fan, he or she would pay thousands for this privilege. Try pretending to yourself that these two people are your billionaire fans.

Make your entrance, read, talk, take questions, exactly as you'd do if there were 20 people, or 200.

Introduction

Once the host has introduced you, walk confidently to your position, smile and thank the host if appropriate. Count silently "one thousand one, one thousand two, one thousand three," before you say anything. Look at your audience. Let your audience look at you. Smile.

If the host forgot to remind people to turn off their phones, you might want to do that now, to minimize the chance of disruptions.

Connecting with your audience

Connecting with an audience is similar to meeting someone for the first time. You smile. You look them in the eyes. You start a conversation along a familiar track, which deepens as trust grows on both sides.

People who have just met tend to drop into conversation when they realize the other person is listening, asking good questions and using open body language—all of which show genuine interest. When you walk on stage, take a moment to pause and "listen" to your audience. Don't ignore them; look at them. Though the words you read are not specifically questions to your audience, they are prompts; their purpose is to arouse thoughts, emotions and memories in the people who hear them.

Read for your audience, not for yourself. Think about your audience, not about yourself. Be interested in the people who have come to hear your words. In your linking remarks, use your social skills: connect with audience members as you would connect with individuals. An audience is only, and always, a collection of individuals.

Some writers jump straight into the reading; others start with a few words of introduction. The latter is a better tactic for beginners, as it gives your audience—and you!—time to settle into the sound of your voice. Since you checked the microphone beforehand, there's no need to tap it and say, "Can you hear me in the back?" Instead, thank your audience for coming, tell them how much you appreciate them being there. A few words of this nature will suffice—and if they can't hear you in the back, they'll let you know. Practice this a few times;

soon you'll be surprised at how easily you'll make these off-the-cuff remarks. Tell your audience the title of your book, if you have one, and perhaps add a sentence or two about the work you're going to read.

Pause. Hold the space in silence for five seconds.

Yes, five seconds. The audience will wait. This is what they came for. And your reading will be more powerful if it's separated from your opening remarks.

Allow yourself to settle into the moment. You'll know when you feel ready. Take your time. Then begin.

Connect first. Read second.

Remember, read slowly! Listen to the meaning and the music of the words. Call up your imaginative circumstances and connect them to your material. Open yourself up to a personal connection with your audience. Hold these connections with conscious intention.

If you notice you're losing your connection to either your material or your audience, pause. Take a sip of water. Recall your imaginative circumstances. Don't worry that your audience will see you making this adjustment. You don't have to be perfect. Being unafraid to allow people to see your human fallibility is what creates intimacy.

When you feel the connection fire again, continue where you left off.

Looking up

Don't bury your face in your book. The audience wants to see your face, and the more eye contact you make or seem to make, the more powerful your reading will be. You've practiced taking your eyes away from the page and returning to the same spot. You've found the thought beats in your text. Give the words you've written space by looking up at your audience.

Look at your listeners as if you were telling a story around your dinner table. Make eye contact with as many people as possible, at different moments. If that freaks you out, choose three spots on the walls just above head height—left, right and center—and direct your eyes there. Nobody will know you're not looking at anyone at all.

In the beginning, you might find this a bit awkward but don't worry, your comfort level will rise quickly from event to event.

Laughter

Laughter is one of the most immediate ways in which your audience shows its approval and adds energy to the room. Never anticipate laughter. Just because you think a line is funny doesn't mean your audience will find it funny. Sometimes your audience will laugh at a line you don't find funny at all—and at the next reading, the same line will pass by in silence. Even so, you'll discover that certain lines consistently get laughs—until the one day when those lines fall flat. Your audience will laugh instead at your comic timing of a serious line, or the way you shrug your shoulders or smile, or your response to a comment from someone in the front row.

Laughter is an expression of happiness; it creates joy and makes people feel good. You don't have to handle it or control it, so don't try to stifle it, don't talk over it. Let it fill the room with warmth and good cheer.

When do you start reading again? We wish it was possible to give you an exact answer to this so that you'll be completely prepared when you encounter your first laughing audience, but we can't. All laughter is different. There's honking, screaming, falling-on-the-floor laughter; and there's chuckling and little satisfied grunts. You'll have to play it by ear. As a general rule, wait for disruptive laughter to subside completely before you continue; start reading again over the tail end of the more controlled, chuckly kind.

Dealing with laughter is as much about play and timing as it is about planning. Your best bet is to simply enjoy it when it happens and surf the wave. Pretty soon, you'll have your balance.

One more thing: don't laugh at your own jokes or funny lines. Let your audience do that for you.

Disruptions

Maybe a siren blares in the street outside, or the electricity goes off, or a motorcycle revs up in the parking lot, or a clumsy back-row onlooker knocks over a vase. It's unnatural to ignore it. Look up, notice it, but minimize it. Don't look annoyed. Don't make a snide or grumpy remark. Smile!

A smile conveys that you and the audience are on the same side. This is an interruption, there's no denying it, but we'll wait patiently together for peace to be restored. If an amusing remark comes to you, great. Every minor disruption gives you a chance to be creative and playful on stage.

You might even be able to work the disruption into your reading. For example, at a Poetry Alive! show for middle school students, I was midway through "Fifteen" by William Stafford—in which a boy finds a motorcycle lying on its side "with engine running" and the rider lying dazed nearby—when a deep-throated rumble came through the open windows. I knew right away it was a Harley. I increased my voice projection as the boy in the poem thought about taking the bike for a spin. The biker outside revved his engine. I revved my voice as the biker in the poem came to and remounted his bike. Luckily for me, the Harley roared off as I reached the line, "He ran his hand / over it, called me a good man, roared away." I stood silently as the bike's roar faded into the distance. When it was gone, I said the last line: "I stood there, fifteen."

If you can be creative around a disruption, your audience will love you for it.

Phones

A ringing cell phone is the most common disruption. When this occurs, and it will, most people will scramble to silence their phone on the first ring. Your best bet is to ignore it and continue with your reading. Occasionally, someone will take a call and walk out of the room to talk. Ignore this too.

If the person takes the call and whispers a conversation, your best move is to stop your reading and say, "Excuse me, would you please take your call outside? Thank you." Wait until the person leaves, make no other comment, then go back to your reading.

If it's your phone—oops, you forgot to turn it off!— keep your cool. How many times did it ring before you realized it was yours? It'll probably stop before you're able to locate it and turn it off. Waiting it out is better than fumbling and floundering—but if you can reach your phone easily and calmly, do so. Apologize to your audience as you wait for the ringing to end, and thank them for having already turned off their phones in advance. You might spot a few people reaching guiltily into their pockets or handbags. Then pick up where you left off, as if the interruption never happened.

People

Sometimes you will encounter a restless child in the audience. Usually parents are responsible and will take a disruptive child out of the room. When this happens, break your reading for a moment to thank the parent for their consideration. If the parent is less considerate, or if the disruption is caused by someone talking loudly near the door, the host should deal with it. If there's no host to deal with it, you'll have to deal with it yourself. You are entirely within your rights to politely ask the parent to take the child outside until it calms down.

Most disruptions pass in a few minutes, so the best approach is to ignore them and continue on. If it's something more dramatic, such as an argument, and the disruptors don't tone it down even after you ask them, announce an intermission.

I've seen very few disruptions that couldn't be handled with a little patience and kindness. You may feel a bit uncomfortable at first dealing so firmly with people. Know that the rest of your audience will appreciate your professionalism, and take heart. It's your reading. You are in charge. After you've encountered a few disruptive bumps, you'll be able to handle these little irritants smoothly.

Hecklers

You are very unlikely to encounter a heckler, but if you do, keep your cool. Remember that your audience came to hear you, not the heckler. Just stop reading and hold your silence. Let the heckler play it out for thirty seconds or so while you assess the situation. If you determine that you have a committed heckler bent on disrupting your reading, your best option is to acknowledge the heckler verbally to your audience and call an intermission, saying something like, "We have a person in the audience who strongly disagrees with what I'm saying. Let's take an intermission while the two of us sort this out. We'll get started again in ten minutes. Thank you."

Over the course of three decades, I've only had to call for an intermission once. A heckler walked onto the stage and demanded I give up the microphone because he had something important to say. After trying to reason with him for a minute or so, I called for an intermission, and we managed to sort it out. This was a poetry slam and I was the host—so your chances of having to deal with a heckler are very slim.

Checking your timing

Discreetly check the time now and then. It's helpful to wear a watch or place one on the podium in case there's no clock visible. Another option is to enlist a friend or the host of a loosely structured event such as a bookstore reading to keep an eye on the time. Have them signal you when you're at the halfway mark. Are you running long or short? You might choose to cut or add material, or simply shorten or lengthen your off-the-cuff remarks.

The Q & A

Most single-author and some shared readings end with a Q & A. If someone is interviewing you, they will field the questions. Sometimes a bookstore manager will join you at this point to field the questions. Usually you'll field them yourself.

In most venues, people will ask questions from their seats without a microphone. Always repeat the question. Even if you could hear it perfectly, that might not be true for the people sitting behind the questioner.

Most questions are friendly; sometimes they can be challenging. The best way to handle an uncomfortable question is to remember that you're in charge. If you'd prefer not to answer it, just say so. Better if you can find a way to deflect the question into more congenial territory; the way to do this is to take a moment, imagine a related, friendly question, and answer that question without looking flustered. Then move on quickly to the next questioner—or if there isn't one, wrap things up firmly. If you lose your cool, the hostile person wins.

In a bigger venue where a microphone is necessary and there's nobody else to field questions, you'll have to walk around the room taking questions with microphone in hand. Inevitably, someone will want to take the microphone from you. Hang on tight and say, "That's okay, I'll hold it for you." The person who holds the microphone controls the room.

Never let an audience member control the room. If someone is using the Q & A as an opportunity to pontificate, or tell their own story, or argue with you, cut them off as politely as you can. If possible, find something in what they said that you can plausibly "answer" even if it wasn't actually a question. Then move on firmly or wrap things up.

Wrapping it up

"Thank you" is all you need to say—but make it genuine and heartfelt. Feel gratitude that these people took time and effort to hear you read and honor them by making eye contact to right, left and center before you move to the signing table or otherwise signify that your reading is over.

If there is not going to be a Q & A, hold silence for five seconds after you finish your last line, then say, "Thank you."

"Thank you" cues your audience to applaud. Applause is their way of thanking you and rewarding you for a job well done. Stand still and accept it. Smile, or even take a bow. Don't rush off the stage. Enjoy your success.

After the reading

If you've connected with your audience during your reading by looking up, being vulnerable and dealing creatively with any disruptions, folks will be more inclined to talk to you afterward, buy your books and add their email addresses to your mailing list. These conversations have great value. You'll acquire new fans and make new friends. You'll inspire people to continue with their writing. They'll inspire you. No matter how digitized we become, good old-fashioned face-to-face communication is still the best way to create an enduring relationship.

It's important that you think of the connection between writer and reader as a relationship if you want to build the audience for your work. Novels, poems and memoirs are vectors of human connection. You are inviting your readers into your imagination and your experience, and they in turn are joining their imagination and experience to yours. Like all relationships, this one requires nurturing.

When you talk to people after your event, make sure you give them your contact information. More importantly, ask for their contact information and permission to add their name and email address to your database. When they start receiving emails from you, they'll remember that moment when you looked up from the signing table, or stood next to them at the drinks table, and noticed them.

Multi-reader programs

Tailoring your reading

Let's say you've planned a reading that leans in an emotionally heavy direction. You're the second of three readers. The first reader's work is emotionally heavier than yours. What do you do?

You might change out your material altogether, to lighten the mood and make your work stand out in contrast. Or you might decide you want to add more weight to what you've planned to read by adding other pieces that are even heavier.

You are under no obligation to change your presentation in order to accommodate other readers. That said, if you see an opportunity to rearrange your material so that you can expand on, reinforce or make a stand against an idea that's being presented by another reader, by all means do so. You'll add a layer of narrative to the entire event that would not have been there otherwise.

When the event is running late

Most events end on time, but some run over. There may have been a late start, or too many readers on the list, or a long-winded host, or readers exceeding their allotted time. You can't control any of these variables, but you can control the length of your own reading.

If you find yourself last in a show that's running late, check with the host to see if it's okay to extend your reading past the agreed-upon end time. Usually you'll find that the audience is happy to stay, but there may be limits on the venue. Ask the host if you need to shorten your reading. If the answer is yes, decide before you start what the cuts will be so you can present your most robust material (which you have already identified in rehearsal and previous performances). Even if the answer is no, have cuts in mind so that if you sense your audience is tired, you can shorten your reading. Throw yourself into it with all the energy you can muster. The audience will pick up your energy and go home satisfied and happy.

You may also be able to control your place in the order of readers. This may sound counterintuitive, but we recommend going first if you can. The first reader never has to worry about the event running long, or losing the audience's attention, or being stressed or tired from waiting. After your turn is over, you can relax. So ask. If the host says no, you've lost nothing.

If the program includes ten or more readers, follow this early-on-the-list strategy but aim for the third or fourth slot. If there's an intermission, the prime slot comes right before it.

MORE ON CONNECTING WITH THE AUDIENCE

I once asked a master storyteller where the story lived. She cupped her hands and said, "The story lives between us in a wool nest. It's my story. It's your story. It's our story." In other words, your writing isn't fully alive until an audience is there to read or hear it.

As we said above, your audience is your ally. They got up off their couches, sat in the subway or drove through traffic, maybe paid some money, all because they want to witness your imagination at work, first-hand. So make your reading all about them.

Frank Sinatra was a master at this. I once saw him in concert at the Sands in Las Vegas. The auditorium had red carpet, soft seats and round tables, just as it must have had back in the days of the Rat Pack. A much older Sinatra walked from behind the curtain that night, and this is what he did:

1. He smiled, bowed and mouthed the words, "Thank you."
2. He blew a kiss.
3. He took his time as he moved to center stage. On his way, he nodded to the band.
4. He opened his arms and bowed again, allowing our applause to wash over him.
5. He said into the microphone, "Thank you, thank you very much, thank you."

All this before he began to sing "I've Got You Under My Skin." Note the choice of song: "you" and "I," tight together.

Increasing intimacy

Susan Batson, who has been teaching actors in New York for over forty years, parses the word "intimacy" as "into-me-see." Allowing someone to see into you, to feel a sense of intimacy with you, is the magic that transforms a listener into a fan. It means peeling back your protective layers and inviting people to look at you, and inside you.

A good reading is like pillow talk. People have come to experience your work up close. They want to hear you whisper, laugh with you, cry with you, learn from you, feel the rhythm of your heart and your thoughts.

Remember that vulnerability does not imply a loss of control. The combination of your vulnerability, your openness, your willingness to be seen, with your confident mastery of the stage and your material is what mesmerizes an audience. And as you become more comfortable in the spotlight, you too will feel the warmth of the intimacy you create by being vulnerable. It may even become an adrenaline rush. You'll come to feel this warmth as a reward for pushing through the loneliest, most despairing moments of your writing.

The spirit of the moment

When the intimacy is flowing between you and your audience, you are in the spirit of the moment: fully present, un-self-conscious yet entirely aware. You're in the zone. You can be spontaneous and relaxed while still holding yourself in stage mode.

Dropping into the spirit of the moment is similar to improvising, but it's not the same. It's about feeling the emotional connection that you've created between yourself and your material, and between yourself and the audience, and feeling comfortable enough to be your authentic self, open and humanly imperfect and vulnerable.

Here are four basic approaches that will build your spirit-of-the-moment chops:

- Be yourself
- Take your time
- Tell personal stories
- Engage the audience

1. Be yourself

Being yourself is the best choice you can make to build your confidence. Play to your strengths. If you're shy, be shy. If you're outgoing, be outgoing. If you're happy, be happy. If you're a miserable curmudgeon, be a miserable curmudgeon. (That might seem a bit odd, but you wouldn't be the first person to make a curmudgeonly persona work for you. Think of Winston Churchill or the comedian George Carlin.)

Observe yourself for five minutes in a full-length mirror. Note your posture. Do you like what you see? If not, how can you change it? Is your body relaxed? How about that smile? The mirror is your friend. Your body is your instrument, and also your director. The more you watch yourself in the mirror, the more you'll start to enjoy what you see.

Another way to practice being yourself is to video yourself. Set your smartphone on a tripod or lean it against a book. Take a moment. Then walk in front of it as if you were walking on stage.

Video yourself for a couple of minutes. Look out the window. Stare into the camera. Note what's on the desk.

Regard the ceiling. Watch your hands while you move them around. I make funny faces when I do this exercise. (You can delete the video later.) If you feel moved to speak do so, but don't if you'd rather not. As we said above, silence can be more compelling than words.

Watch your video four or five times. You'll see yourself in action being yourself. You'll also notice when you're affecting movements or patterns of speech that aren't truly you. I tend to default to a public persona of "lively performer on stage" when I'm feeling insecure about showing my true self, which is more thoughtful, less dramatic. Once you've identified your own default settings for covering up insecurity and nerves, you can weed them out.

Being yourself is an ongoing project. Fred Rogers, who hosted the classic children's TV show *Mr. Rogers' Neighborhood*, closed every episode by saying, "There's no person in the world like you and I like you just the way you are." One of the reasons for Mr. Rogers' success was that he was committed to being himself on stage and off, even when he was appearing before the Senate Subcommittee on Communication. You can find his exchange with Senator Pastore—a great example of someone making a curmudgeonly persona work for him—on YouTube. It's an incredible example of the power of authenticity.

2. Take your time

When you take your time, you give yourself room to think, to be and to come up with off-the-cuff things to say.

One of the most valuable rehearsal notes I ever

received was from the theater director David Behrstock. For some reason, I was in a hurry. Maybe I was hungry and thinking about lunch. "Stop right there," David said. "Don't say another word. You're talking too fast. You're emotionally disconnected."

He went on to give me the advice which we've already given you: whenever you start to feel yourself disconnecting emotionally from your material, stop right where you are, even if you're in mid-sentence. Hold your pause until you reconnect emotionally. Take as long as you like: 10 seconds, 20 seconds, even 30 seconds isn't too much. Being confident in your vulnerability endears you to your audience. Then change your position and pick up where you left off.

3. Tell personal stories

Personal stories invite your audience to connect with you by giving them a chance to learn how you think, what matters to you and how you interact with the world. So when an opening appears, trust your personal stories. You might remark on how your book was inspired by a lifelong romantic fantasy, or you might tell your audience how a character or a poem took you by surprise.

Just because these stories are personal, told in your own voice, doesn't mean you haven't rehearsed them! Rehearsal gives you the confidence that you will tell your story well. But keep it casual and personal, not "written up."

For example, when I'm reading my poems about the early years of the poetry slam, I often tell a brief story about a slam poet named Maverick. Unlike most slam poets, who moved around and waved their arms while performing their material from memory, Maverick read sitting on a stool like a 1940s' torch singer. Audiences loved her and judges always gave her high scores.

Be concise. If you feel yourself rambling, simply stop and move on to your next piece. Or:

4. Engage the audience

If you feel the energy of your event sagging, you might choose to follow a comment or a little personal story with a rhetorical question to the audience. For example, if you're reading a piece about growing up in a working-class family, you might preface it by saying, "My father worked for the power company; my mother was a nurse. How many of you remember your mother or father leaving for work at the crack of dawn?"

When you drop into the spirit of the moment with spontaneous moves such as this, your audience will drop in too. When they do, they'll likely surprise you with all kinds of responses, such as unexpected laughter.

BOOKING AND PROMOTING YOUR READING

Since a vital part of a successful reading is getting people into seats, we'd like to spend some time on the logistics of setting one up.

Starting out

Nobody knows you're available for an event unless you tell them. You might feel a little timid at first—that's normal. You'll soon find that most people who arrange readings are looking for talent. Especially well-rehearsed, skilled talent like you.

Begin by asking a trusted friend to help you organize a reading for friends, like a house concert. Start small, with four or five people—more if you feel comfortable. Friends support friends, so they will turn out for your debut reading. They'll enjoy being able to say, "I was there at the start." This also gives you the chance to get some video of yourself in action.

You can then reach out to local literary organizations, schools, colleges, retreat centers, churches (depending on your material), nursing homes and social organizations such as the Rotary Club. And bookstores—even if you don't have a book. Many bookstores host open mics.

Whoever you contact will want to check out you and your work online. So before you go public, get your digital platform up and running.

Your digital platform

Emily Dickinson didn't have a platform and look what happened to her—she got famous after she died. If you're cool with this, fine. If you'd like some recognition during your lifetime, you need to get the word out.

In the nineteenth century, platforms were the printing press and the lecture circuit. In the second decade of the twenty-first century, the digital space has the most reach. Twenty years from now, other platforms will probably exist. In order to sell yourself (yes, we said "sell"—you're selling your writing, and you're selling your reading too), you have to play on the field that's available. Right now, a digital platform is essential for building your writing career.

You should have:

- A website
- A Facebook author page
- Twitter, Instagram and/or LinkedIn accounts
- An email mailing list

If you already have a digital platform, make sure it's up to date. If you can afford to hire someone to help you, do so; the cost may be less than you expect. If your budget requires that you do it yourself, you'll find plenty of tutorials on YouTube.

For most people, Facebook is the easiest place to start. A Facebook author page is not the same thing as a regular Facebook page. It's a place where strangers can follow what you post about your writing without you having to accept them as "friends" who see your personal posts. Current Facebook rules mean that your new author page won't show up in search results until 100 people like it, so once it's up, you'll need to beg your friends to help you out.

Next, your website. Wordpress, Squarespace and Wix make it easy to build a site yourself. The site should include video of you reading your work; samples of your work; links to online retailers of your book or books; quotes from reviews or other writers; an "Events" page for upcoming readings (try not to have it empty—even if you schedule a reading for your cat); a bio or, better, a downloadable press kit which should include three high-resolution photos—a head shot and two of you in an onstage setting; and a contact form.

Experiment with Twitter, LinkedIn, Instagram and the many other social media outlets available to you. Some people find that Twitter fits their style. Others prefer Instagram. If you're a business author, LinkedIn is valuable. You'll find a graduate school of good material online which will help you devise the best strategy for maximizing your social media efforts.

The final item, a mailing list, can be managed through websites such as MailChimp and Constant Contact. Start building it by adding a call-to-action button on your website that invites visitors to add their name to your mailing list. You can be sure that someone who takes this action wants to know more about you. It's better to have 100 people who have signed up voluntarily than a huge mailing list of strangers who will delete your email unopened.

Don't deluge people with emails, but do send out an occasional newsletter or announce something big such as the publication of a book. Knowing where people live enables you to let them know if you'll be doing an event in their area. A column for how you met the person comes in useful if they reply to your email and you want to reply to them.

As director of the Taos Storytelling Festival, I'm tasked with finding two first-rate storytellers every year. Like most producers, I start with personal recommendations. Once I have a list of names, I review their online presence. If I land on a website that looks like it was built ten years ago and hasn't been revised since, I reject that candidate. But if the website is current and well designed and has a press packet, I look at the content, especially videos. Content is more important than production quality—but high production values make an impact and can often swing the decision in your favor. On the other hand, a great storyteller who posts lots of DIY-quality videos taken in various venues is also desirable because I can see they're actively promoting themselves, which makes my job easier.

It takes me about five minutes to decide if a storyteller is in the running. An up-to-date digital platform tells me that, if I hire that storyteller, they will promote the Taos Storytelling Festival through their network. A phone conversation seals the deal.

Getting a commitment

Once you start identifying people who might book you, get their contact information. Whether they approached you or you approached them, it's your job to follow up. Never rely on them to follow up with you.

Ask people whom you meet in person or in a phone conversation if they would like you to add their name to your mailing list. Permission is required to conform with current privacy regulations, and verbal permission is enough. Even the most well-intentioned person you meet at a networking event will forget to go to your website and add their address. But you won't forget since it's to your advantage to make sure you stay in contact with them. And once you have permission, you have a good reason to contact them again.

In your first email to your new contact, let them know you've added them to your mailing list, and (if appropriate) give them a heads-up that they will be receiving regular newsletters from you. Most importantly, request a phone meeting to discuss when you might read at their venue. If the call goes well, they'll probably tell you that they need to check the date with colleagues. Ask when would be a good time to call back, and put that date in your calendar so you don't forget.

It takes, on average, 12 contacts over two to six months to secure a booking. Figure on another 4–8 contacts after that to settle logistics (including your fee if applicable), concluding with a last text, call or email to confirm you are on the way to the venue. When you stay on top of these contact points, the host will appreciate your professionalism. After the show, along with your thank-you note, you can ask them to recommend you for other events nearby or in areas where you may plan to be in the future.

Personal touches such as phone calls, small gifts and thank-you notes will set you apart, because most people rely almost solely on their digital platform.

FOR PUBLISHED AUTHORS

Don't just leave it to your publisher's publicity department. They're busy, and you're probably not one of their big fish. Most of us aren't.

It's a good idea to forge relationships with your local bookstores, especially independent ones. Expand your definition of "local" as far as seems reasonable. For example, in New Mexico, where there are few towns spaced widely apart, a bookstore 150 miles away can count as local. Even in a metropolis such as New York, where "local" is a much tighter concept, many independent bookstores will consider you local if you live within the city or close by. You can strengthen this connection by dropping in occasionally and offering to sign stock or supply copies on consignment.

If independent booksellers like your book, they will hand-sell it to their clientele. These people are in the business because they love books, not because it's a money-making machine; they love having direct contact with authors and they appreciate your appreciation of the work they do.

So, set up local events yourself. As well as bookstores, look for literary societies, writers' groups and lunch clubs. If there is no obvious venue where you live, arrange a reading at an art gallery or café. If you spring for a case of wine you can call it a launch party and more people will come. You could also hold an event at a bar, where people can buy their own drinks—but make sure you have a quiet space for your reading, or can take over the bar for an hour or so (maybe before the usual opening time), as people who are not there for your party aren't going to stop talking.

If you're using a non-bookstore venue, you may have to badger your publishers to make sure there are enough copies of your book for sale. Reckon on one-third of the number of guests you're expecting. Sales of copies sent directly from the publishers don't show up in sales figures, so sell your complimentary copies and then buy replacements with the money you've just taken.

In recognition of the effort you're putting in, ask the publisher to send further complimentary copies for promotional purposes. You're going to make more efficient use of them than anyone.

Book tour

Publishers don't want to spend money on airfares and hotels, so they will be unwilling to send you out on book tour unless they think you will draw a sizable crowd. Even if they do send you out on tour, don't rely on them to publicize the events. Your own mailing list, and friends, will generate far more occupied seats. Send personalized emails at least two weeks before the event, and again the week before. It's time-consuming labor, but it's the best way to bring people out.

Consider recruiting a local friend, ideally a writer or media personality with a following, to be "in conversation" with you—in other words, to interview you about your book as part of the event. Another idea is to share a reading with a local author whose audience is similar to yours; you can both read a few passages and "interview" each other. Either way, you'll increase the pool of people who are likely to come and reach strangers who would never hear of you otherwise.

If you do this, meet with the other person in advance

and decide what questions will be asked. You don't need to script the discussion, but make notes of the talking points you each want to hit.

Above all, choose someone you trust to be professional. You don't want them hogging the limelight, turning up unprepared or springing an unpleasant surprise on you just for a laugh.

Live-stream the event

In the age of social media, the actual number of people in the audience is less important than broadcasting it. However, live-streaming is not appropriate for all events. If you're doing an open mic or other hosted event, check with the organizer first.

Live-streaming on a platform such as Facebook has many benefits:

- Your book tour has much wider impact—even if people don't actually watch the video, they see that it's happening.
- More people can "attend" the event as it happens.
- The video is archived so that it can be viewed later. (But beware: the quality isn't good enough for your website or YouTube. For that, you'll need to video the event directly on your phone or tablet.)
- You can use the video for training, as athletes do, by watching yourself in action.

One author friend had 12 people in the bookstore for

her first live-streamed event, and 88 people watching on Facebook. That's a 100-person reading, which wouldn't have taken place at all if the publishers had thought that only 12 people would turn up.

Furthermore, on social media every event looks like a success. The more events you have, the bigger a success your book looks—regardless of how many people actually turn up to them. (You won't see the audience in the video.) This is an argument for doing as many events as you can arrange, regardless of your expected audience.

How to live-stream on Facebook

Log into Facebook on your device. Select "Live." Position the device; depending on what kind of stand you use, you may have to switch the camera to selfie mode. Hit start. When you're done, hit stop and then "Post" if you want it to stay on your page. It's that simple.

Frame the picture so that it's tight on you, or you and whomever you're in conversation with. Crop out the audience: backs of heads look bad, and this way it doesn't matter if only two people and a dog turn up. Most bookstores have a ladder, which will position your device high enough, and book stands to hold it upright. You may need to secure your phone to the stand with an elastic band to get a straight-on angle.

Live-streaming sucks battery, so you'll need your power cord. Bring a 10-foot extension cord in case there isn't an outlet nearby.

Give yourself plenty of time to sort all this out before your audience starts to arrive.

*

As with any craft, the more you read in public—or in private, as part of your editing process—the better you'll get at it. If you are comfortable reading for an audience, you will find far more opportunities to publicize your work. You will convert even accidental listeners into fans.

You are also your own audience. If you develop your reading chops, you will develop your listening chops as well. You will gain a perspective on your writing that you never thought possible, and it will improve in ways that amaze you. We promise you that.

This book is also available in e-book, audiobook and downloadable pdf formats. Please visit twice5miles.com for details on these and other Twice 5 Miles titles.

If you enjoyed this book, please post a review on the website of your favorite online retailer.

37195671R00057

Made in the USA
Middletown, DE
23 February 2019